*Music*

7-99

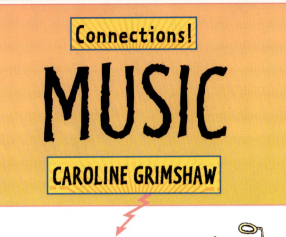

# Connections!

# MUSIC

## CAROLINE GRIMSHAW

MUSIC CONSULTANT
**CHARLES SHAAR MURRAY**
COGNITIVE CONSULTANT
**ANTHONY BLAKE**
THANKS TO **ANDREW KUROWSKI**

**WORLD BOOK**
In association with
**TWO-CAN**

# Connections!

# MUSIC

CREATIVE AND EDITORIAL DIRECTOR
CONCEPT/FORMAT/DESIGN/TEXT
**CAROLINE GRIMSHAW**

MUSIC CONSULTANT
**CHARLES SHAAR MURRAY**

COGNITIVE CONSULTANT
**ANTHONY BLAKE**
THANKS TO **ANDREW KUROWSKI**

ILLUSTRATIONS
**NICK DUFFY** ☆ **SPIKE GERRELL** ☆ **JO MOORE**

THANKS TO
**LYNDSEY PRICE** PICTURE RESEARCH
**CLAIRE YUDE** AND **BRONWEN LEWIS** EDITORIAL SUPPORT
**IQBAL HUSSAIN** TEXT
AND **ROBERT FRIPP** ☆ **PAUL DU NOYER**
**TIM SANPHER** ☆ **ANDREW JARVIS**

**TITLES IN THIS SERIES** →
☆ PEOPLE
☆ BUILDINGS
☆ EARTH
☆ ART
☆ MUSIC

FIRST PUBLISHED IN THE UNITED STATES IN 1996 BY
WORLD BOOK, INC.
525 W. MONROE
20TH FLOOR
CHICAGO, IL USA 60661
IN ASSOCIATION WITH TWO-CAN PUBLISHING LTD.

COPYRIGHT © CAROLINE GRIMSHAW 1996

FOR INFORMATION ON OTHER WORLD BOOK PRODUCTS,
CALL 1-800-255-1750, X 2238.

ISBN: 0-7166-1760-9 (PBK.)  ISBN: 0-7166-1759-5 (HBK.)
LC: 96-60457

PRINTED IN HONG KONG
1 2 3 4 5 6 7 8 9 10 99 98 97 96

# Contents

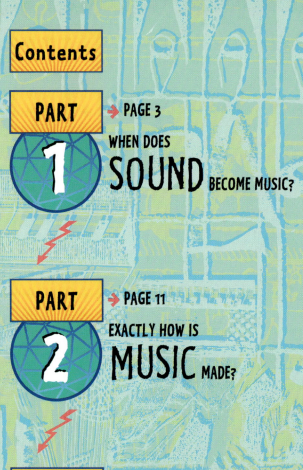

**DISCOVER THE CONNECTIONS THROUGH QUESTIONS AND ANSWERS...**
YOU CAN READ THIS BOOK FROM START TO FINISH OR
LEAP-FROG THROUGH THE SECTIONS
FOLLOWING THE PATHS SUGGESTED
IN THESE SPECIAL "CONNECT! BOXES."

**ENJOY YOUR JOURNEY OF
DISCOVERY AND UNDERSTANDING**

We hear it all around us everyday. Now it's time to ask yourself...

When does

# sound

become music?

## What is music?

## Does the world need music?

## Who makes music around the world?

All these questions (and many more!) will be answered in PART ONE of your journey of discovery and understanding. Just turn the page! --->

# 1 What is music?

Music is a collection of sounds that are arranged into patterns. These sounds, or notes, may be produced by human voices, instruments or even nature itself. Music plays an important part in people's lives around the world.

## People enjoy making music and listening to it because...

**1** MUSIC MOVES US A powerful piece of music can affect people's emotions. An audience at an opera may find some songs, or arias as they are called, so moving that they cry.

**2** MUSIC BRINGS PEOPLE TOGETHER Music can be a shared experience. Pop and classical concerts sometimes attract thousands of devoted fans.

**3** MUSIC HELPS PEOPLE EXPRESS HOW THEY FEEL Some musicians capture the imagination of people all over the world. A few are remembered long after they have died, such as **WOLFGANG AMADEUS MOZART** (1756–91).

**4** MUSIC GIVES US SOME IDEA ABOUT HOW OTHER PEOPLE LIVE Music allows us to learn about different cultures. The sounds made, the instruments used and the messages in the music and words all give us clues about other people's worlds.

**Connect!** WHY DO SOME COMPOSERS BECOME LEGENDS, WHILE OTHERS ARE FORGOTTEN? TO FIND OUT TURN TO Q54.

**Connect!** MUSIC GIVES PEOPLE THE CHANCE TO SHARE THEIR OPINIONS WITH OTHERS. TURN TO Q46.

# 2 When does sound become music?

When sound, or noise, is organized or manipulated by a person into some kind of pattern it may become music.

THIS COLLECTION OF SOUNDS MAY EMOTIONALLY MOVE THE LISTENER. IT MAY MEAN SOMETHING TO THE PERSON WHO MADE IT, BUT ABSOLUTELY NOTHING TO ANYONE ELSE!

**TRAFFIC SOUND IS AN EVENT** You hear it and it reminds you to take care when crossing the road. But if this "noise" is recorded and combined with other sounds it may become part of a composer's musical work.

☆ **A COMPOSER CHOOSES A VARIETY OF SOUNDS AND COMBINES THEM TO CREATE MUSIC...**

The sounds selected and the way they are combined will depend on many things...

TRADITION ➡ ⬅ THE COMPOSER'S EXPERIENCE

THE INSTRUMENTS AVAILABLE ➡ ⬅ THE MUSIC'S FUNCTION

**DATE** 29 AUGUST 1969. **VENUE** SAN FRANCISCO. The composer **ROBERT MORAN** stunned the musical world when he aired his latest work, *30 Minutes for 39 Autos.* The instrumental stars of the piece were not violins or pianos, but 39 motor cars. Moran "conducted" the vehicles' horns and lights and combined them with the sound of a synthesizer to produce his half-hour extravaganza.

**Connect!** SOME PEOPLE CREATE MUSIC USING SOUNDS MADE BY WHATEVER OBJECTS THEY CAN LAY THEIR HANDS ON! SEE Q27.

## Music is all around us...

IT IS PLAYED IN SOME SHOPPING CENTERS.

SOME PEOPLE LISTEN TO MUSIC WHILE THEY WORK.

IT IS PART OF TELEVISION PROGRAMS AND FILMS.

WE MAY PLAY MUSIC AS WE TRAVEL IN OUR CARS.

IT IS PLAYED IN OUR HOMES ON OUR RADIOS AND STEREO SYSTEMS.

WE MAY HEAR MUSIC AS WE WALK AROUND OUR NEIGHBORHOOD.

### Prove It!

Keep a musical diary for one week, noting every time you hear a piece of music. What was the music like? Where did you hear it? How did it make you feel?

WHAT MAY SEEM STRANGE IN ONE COUNTRY, SOUNDS PERFECTLY NORMAL TO PEOPLE IN ANOTHER.

## Different countries may have unique styles...

Just as people around the world speak different languages, so different countries have developed their own traditional kinds of music and instruments.

### ☆ SPAIN
**INSTRUMENT**
Acoustic guitar.
**FEATURES**
Six nylon strings and a body made from various woods, such as cedar, walnut and maple. The guitar often accompanies flamenco dancers.

### ☆ INDIA
**INSTRUMENT**
Sitar.
**FEATURES**
Seven metal strings, a wooden body, and between 11 and 19 strings, called "sympathetic," which vibrate when the main strings are plucked.

### ☆ CHINA
**INSTRUMENT**
Pipa.
**FEATURES**
Four silk, or nylon, strings and a body made of paulownia wood. The pipa is often used to provide the music for traditional storytelling.

### ☆ MONGOLIA
**INSTRUMENT**
Khur.
**FEATURES**
Two horsehair strings which are played with a bow, and a wooden body which is covered with catskin.

☆ THE STORY OF MUSIC IS A COMPLICATED ONE AND IT CHANGES AND MOVES ON EVERY DAY.

### Connect!
SEE HOW PEOPLE AROUND THE WORLD USE MUSIC IN Q11.

## QUESTION 3

# How do we hear music?

### We hear and make sense of soundwaves.

When a musical note is played, a small part of the instrument begins to vibrate. This makes the air around it vibrate as well. The vibrations produce a pattern of soundwaves, which travel through the air to our ears. Once there, the waves cause the eardrums to vibrate in the same pattern. The brain interprets the vibrations and puts the sound together as a musical note.

IT IS THE SPEED OF THE VIBRATIONS THAT DETERMINES WHAT A NOTE SOUNDS LIKE—THE FASTER THEY ARE, THE HIGHER THE NOTE.

### ☆ HEARING SOUND

**1** Plucking a guitar string causes it to vibrate. The air around the string also vibrates.

**2** The vibrations form soundwaves, which collect in the ear flap. These pass down the ear canal to the eardrum.

**3** The three tiny bones behind the eardrum pick up the vibrations, amplify them and relay them to the inner ear.

**4** The snail-shaped cochlea, which is full of fluid, converts the vibrations into electric impulses.

**5** The signals travel along the nerves to the brain, where they are interpreted as sound.

### ☆ SEEING SOUND

Each instrument's soundwave produces tiny variations in air pressure. These can be shown as curved lines called waveforms.

SINGLE NOTE PLAYED ON VIOLIN = JAGGED WAVEFORM

SINGLE NOTE PLAYED ON FLUTE = CURVED WAVEFORM

SINGLE NOTE PLAYED ON GONG = IRREGULAR WAVEFORM

### Connect!
WHETHER WE LIKE MUSIC DEPENDS ON OUR TASTE, EXPERIENCE AND MOOD. SEE Q39.

☆ WHEN WE HEAR A POP SONG, THE EARS RECEIVE THE COMBINED SOUNDWAVES FROM ALL THE INSTRUMENTS AND VOICES, MAKING THE EARDRUMS VIBRATE IN A COMPLICATED PATTERN.

## QUESTION 4

# Should music sound pleasant?

(AND WHAT IS PLEASANT?)

Music has a number of functions. Not all music is made to entertain and please the listener. Anyway, what appeals to one person may be jarring to another.

### Connect!

READ ABOUT HOW PEOPLE USE MUSIC IN Q10 AND Q11.

Different cultures, and individuals within those cultures, have their own ideas and thoughts about what is acceptable, pleasant and stimulating. Music that doesn't fit into these rules may be thought to be noise by other people.

### Connect!

WE CAN EXAMINE MUSIC BY LOOKING AT ITS RHYTHM, PITCH AND TONE. TURN TO Q9 TO FIND OUT MORE.

## The East and the West...

With most music in Western countries, two or more musical notes are played together according to certain rules. This pleasing combination of notes is known as harmony. Eastern music often does not obey the same rules. There is no harmony or regular rhythm in traditional Japanese and Chinese music. Indian musicians use instruments which appear exotic and strange.

THE GREEK COMPOSER IANNIS XENAKIS (BORN 1922) IS FAMOUS FOR HIS NON-MELODIC ORCHESTRAL PIECES.

⬆ Japanese drummers.

### Prove It!

Turn the dial on a radio and decide what is music and what is noise. Then ask your friends to do the same. Do you all agree on your choices?

## QUESTION 5

# Do other creatures make music?

Yes, humans are not alone in creating music.

### ☆ WHALES AND DOLPHINS

Whalesong largely consists of grunts and sighs. The low, booming songs of the blue whale can travel through the oceans for over 500 miles. Dolphins use sound to detect objects in the water. They produce loud clicks which bounce off the object and cause vibrations. The dolphin picks up these vibrations and is able to work out the size and distance of the object.

⬆ Dolphins have a range of around 30 sounds, including whistles and clicks.

### ☆ BIRDS

One of the most common sounds in nature is that of birds singing. Their songs range from the simple repetition of one or two notes to highly complex compositions. But why do birds sing the dawn chorus? Scientists believe it helps birds communicate, defend their territory and attract mates.

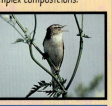

⬆ Male sedge warblers sing elaborate songs to charm females, who are attracted only by the most complicated song.

### ☆ WHAT OTHER NON-HUMAN MUSIC IS THERE?

THERE ARE "SINGING SANDS" AT OVER 30 DESERT SITES AROUND THE WORLD. THE "SINGING" OCCURS WHEN THE GRAINS OF SAND SLIDE AGAINST EACH OTHER.

THE ANCIENT GREEKS THOUGHT THE WHOLE UNIVERSE WAS A MUSICAL INSTRUMENT. THEY BELIEVED THE STARS AND PLANETS WERE FIXED ONTO BLACK SPHERES NESTLED INSIDE EACH OTHER. AS THE SPHERES TURNED THEY WERE SAID TO HUM, PRODUCING THE "MUSIC OF THE SPHERES."

### Prove It!

Listen carefully to a bird singing. Can you detect different songs? Does the bird repeat groups of notes or whole tunes?

### Connect!

MANY COMPOSERS ARE FASCINATED BY THE SOUNDS OF NATURE. SEE Q28.

## QUESTION 6

# Have humans always made music?

The first music was probably made by prehistoric man producing pleasing sounds by banging stone tools together in a regular pattern.

☆ WHICH CAME FIRST—LANGUAGE OR MUSIC? LET'S TAKE A LOOK AT TWO THEORIES...

**1** Some people think that humans tried to communicate long before language developed, by using musical sounds such as the beat of a stone on rock. In this way, music may have been the first means of human communication.

**2** Other people think that singing may have been a halfway step between grunts and the first words. Early societies may have used basic songs (probably with no words) to express their feelings. Singing together encouraged the group to bond.

MUSIC WAS VERY IMPORTANT IN MANY OF THE WORLD'S ANCIENT CIVILIZATIONS. IT WAS USED ON MANY SPECIAL OCCASIONS, SUCH AS RELIGIOUS AND ROYAL CEREMONIES, BANQUETS, PLAYS AND FUNERALS.

| WHEN | WHO | FAVORITE INSTRUMENTS |
|---|---|---|
| 5,000 years ago | Egyptians | Harps, zithers, flutes, castanets |
| 2,500 years ago | Greeks | Lyres, trumpets, horns, oboes |
| 2,000 years ago | Romans | Cymbals, gongs, trumpets |

**Connect!**

SOME MUSIC TODAY STILL FOCUSES ON THE SOUND THAT A VOICE PRODUCES, RATHER THAN ON WORDS. SEE Q35.

## QUESTION 7

# Did early music imitate nature?

Probably, yes.

Humans instinctively need to communicate. Babies learn that by copying certain sounds and ignoring others, they can make themselves understood. In order to make music and communicate, our ancestors may have tried to imitate the sounds of the ocean, the wind, rain, thunder, fire, birdsong and animal cries.

**Connect!**

THERE ARE SOME INSTRUMENTS THAT RELY ON THE WIND TO MAKE THEM WORK. TURN TO Q20.

## QUESTION 8

# Why do we label musical styles?

Labels allow us to see how the many styles of music made around the world differ, and also how they relate to each other.

☆ WE OFTEN DIVIDE MUSIC INTO TWO CATEGORIES...

## Western music

This is the label given to certain styles of music created in Europe, the Americas and Australia. Most Western music is described as either classical or popular.

**CLASSICAL MUSIC COMES IN MANY FORMS:**
● **SYMPHONY** = A complicated composition for the orchestra, usually in four separate sections called movements.
EXAMPLE: *SYMPHONY NO 4*, BY **FELIX MENDELSSOHN** (1809-47).
● **ORATORIO** = Dramatic music based on a religious theme, with solo singers, a chorus and an orchestra.
EXAMPLE: *MESSIAH*, BY **GEORGE FRIDERIC HANDEL** (1685-1759).
● **SONATA** = A composition in three or four movements, usually for a piano, or a piano and one other instrument.
EXAMPLE: *PIANO SONATA IN B MINOR*, BY **FRANZ LISZT** (1811-86).

**POPULAR (OR POP) MUSIC GENERALLY APPEALS TO MANY PEOPLE AT ANY GIVEN TIME IN HISTORY. THERE ARE MANY SUBDIVISIONS OF THIS CATEGORY, FOR EXAMPLE:**
● **COUNTRY AND WESTERN** = Originating from North America, often accompanied by a guitar, fiddle or banjo.
● **FOLK** = Traditional music originating from rural communities, which passes through the centuries from generation to generation.
● **TECHNO** = Largely generated by computers and drum machines, with repeated words, electronic beeps and a thumping beat.
● **HEAVY METAL** = Often played at a loud volume, accompanied by screeching electric guitars and thrashing drums.

## World music

This label describes music made largely by people who live outside of Europe, the Americas and Australia. These cultures have their own styles of classical and popular music.

**INDIA** Traditional Indian music originated in Hindu temples and the royal courts. Popular music is used in Indian films.
INSTRUMENTS: Sitar (a type of stringed instrument), tabla (a pair of small drums), flute.

**AFRICA** Music is important in people's daily activities, especially religious ceremonies and festivals.
INSTRUMENTS: Drums (made of wood, metal, dried vegetables, clay or animal skins), xylophone, iron bells.

**Connect!**

CHECK OUT Q55 TO SEE HOW ONE MUSICIAN COMBINES WESTERN AND WORLD MUSIC.

## QUESTION 9

# How do we describe music?

The combined sounds that make up music can be looked at in various ways. These ways help us to describe what music actually sounds like. Here are some examples...

☆ **RHYTHM**
THE BEAT, OR PULSE, OF A PIECE OF MUSIC.

☆ **TEMPO**
THE SPEED THAT THE MUSIC IS PLAYED AT.

☆ **PITCH**
HOW HIGH OR LOW THE MUSIC SOUNDS.

☆ **TONE**
THE QUALITY OR STRENGTH OF THE SOUND.

### Melody
THE COMPOSER ARRANGES NOTES IN PATTERNS TO CREATE TUNES. THE MOST POIGNANT SEQUENCE IS THE MELODY.

**Prove It!**
Your heart beats to a rhythm as it pumps blood around the body. Feel the beats by touching the inside of your wrist or the side of your neck.

**Connect!**
TURN TO Q12 AND Q13 TO FIND OUT HOW MUSICIANS WRITE DOWN MUSIC.

**Connect!**
SOME COMPOSERS HAVE EXPERIMENTED WITH UNUSUAL RHYTHM, TIMING AND TONE. CHECK OUT Q40 AND Q53.

## QUESTION 10

# Does the world need music?

Of course—and here are some reasons why!

**MUSIC ENTERTAINS US**
The Victorians liked to gather round the piano and have a rousing sing-along. In April 1990 a record-breaking 184,000 people paid to see Paul McCartney and his band perform.

**MUSIC STIMULATES US**
Aerobics and fitness classes usually take place with a pounding pop beat in the background. This helps people move to a rhythm.

**MUSIC RELAXES US**
Certain kinds of music can have a calming effect on us. Babies are lulled to sleep with gentle lullabies.

**SOME PEOPLE SAY THAT MUSIC BRINGS THEM CLOSER TO GOD**
All cultures have religious music. Gospel music, which developed in the 1920s in the black Baptist churches of the US south, can be deeply moving.

**MUSIC ALERTS US, CALLS US AND ACTS AS A SIGNAL**
Priests in Japanese temples call people to prayer by striking huge bells. The bells have no clapper, so they need to be hit on the side with a wooden beam to make a sound.

**MUSIC ALLOWS US TO EXPRESS OPINIONS AND BELIEFS**
In the late 1970s a new form of music called "punk" became popular. The aggressive songs reflected the angry and disillusioned feelings of some of the young people of the time.

**MUSIC MAKES US LAUGH**
Musicals, or musical comedies, use words, songs and dances to tell stories. They first became popular in the US in the late 1800s, because they were entertaining to watch and usually very humorous.

**MUSIC SHOWS US HOW THE WORLD HAS CHANGED**
The formality of 19th century life in Europe was reflected in its classical music and dance. Today, there are less rigid rules telling people how to enjoy themselves.

☆ 1896   ☆ 1996

**Connect!**
MUSIC HELPS US TO TELL STORIES. ONE OF THE BEST EXAMPLES OF THIS IS PETER AND THE WOLF, BY THE RUSSIAN COMPOSER SERGEI PROKOFIEV (1891–1953). EACH CHARACTER IS REPRESENTED BY ITS OWN INSTRUMENT AND MELODY.

**Connect!**
WHAT IS OPERA? FIND OUT THE ANSWER IN Q33.

**Connect!**
TODAY CONCERTS CAN BE BEAMED BY SATELLITE AROUND THE WORLD. SEE HOW THIS AFFECTS MUSIC IN Q52.

# Who makes music around the world?

**Music is important to those who make it, listen to it and use it. Anyone can make music. Examine this musical map.**

**1 AFRICA** Many Africans believe music can be used to communicate with the gods. Bells are rung to protect buildings from ghosts, and witch doctors beat drums to summon spirits. Complicated drum rhythms accompany songs and dances.

**2 AMAZON** The flute is a sacred instrument for the many tribes who live in the rainforests. The men of the Xingu tribe play large, wooden instruments as a way of talking to their gods. The Amazonian Indians play flutes with their noses, by blowing through them with one nostril.

**3 AUSTRALIA** Native Aborigines play unusual instruments, such as the didgeridoo. This is a type of wooden trumpet made from a hollow tree branch over 39 inches long. The musician sings and blows into it to produce a rich drone.

**4 CHINA** Chinese music is more than 2,000 years old. Early orchestras performed at elaborate religious and court ceremonies with hundreds of musicians taking part.

**5 EUROPE** Music plays an important part in worship in Christian churches. Early religious music was called plainsong. The most famous form is the Gregorian Chant, named after Pope Gregory I (AD 540–604).

**6 INDIA** The traditional music, or raga, was originally played in the courts of the great kings. Small orchestras may include a singer, a vina (stringed instrument) and tabla (drums).

**Connect!** HOW ELSE IS MUSIC USED IN RELIGIOUS CEREMONIES? SEE Q42.

**Connect!** INDIAN MUSIC INVOLVES IMPROVIZATION. TO FIND OUT MORE SEE Q37.

**11 RUSSIAN FEDERATION** The bandura—a lute with 36 strings, held vertically on the lap—is popular in Ukrainian orchestras. The triangle-shaped balalaika often accompanies folk songs and dances.

**7 INDONESIA** Gamelan bands make music with hypnotic rhythms. Villagers use hand-made instruments such as bonang (chiming gongs), gambang (xylophones) and drums to accompany puppet plays.

**12 SOUTH AMERICA** Panpipes are popular in Brazil, Peru and Bolivia. They are made from pipes of different lengths joined together side by side, and played by blowing across the top of each pipe.

**Connect!** WESTERN COMPOSERS HAVE BEEN INFLUENCED BY THIS MUSIC. TURN TO Q36.

**8 JAPAN** The traditional court music is called "gagaku." It dates back 1,300 years, and is still played at the imperial palace today. The orchestra includes shakuhachi (bamboo flutes), drums and gongs.

**9 MIDDLE EAST and NORTH AFRICA** Arabic songs are accompanied by flutes, drums and stringed instruments such as the oud and the qanun. The main religious music is the prayer-call, sung from minarets by criers called muezzins.

**10 NORTH AMERICA** The American Indians use music as part of rituals, such as trying to bring down rain or helping hunters make a kill. Medicine men sing while treating the sick. Drums and rattles are the main instruments.

## Prove It!

Make your own panpipes. Take 30 straws and cut each one so that it is shorter than the last one. Arrange them in a row in size order and join them together with sticky tape. Blow across the top—the shorter the straw, the higher the sound.

# 12

# How do we write down music?

Written music is like a route map, or a set of instructions for a journey. It is a diagram which shows a musician how a piece of music should be played.

In the 9th century, European monks would scribble a few basic signs in their prayer books to help them remember the holy songs they sang. Gradually, as the songs became more complicated, the symbols, which had started off as simple reminders, became exact guides to reading and playing music. The way we write down music today dates from around AD 1200.

## ☆ SCALES

● Most Western music is based on scales—a sequence of notes arranged according to rising or falling pitch.

● Notes are labelled A, B, C, D, E, F and G. This cycle of seven letters is repeated.

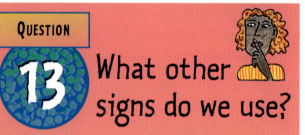

● The distance between a note and the next highest or lowest note with the same letter, for example "C" to "C", is called an octave.

## ☆ THE STAFF

This grid of five lines and four spaces is called the staff or stave. The pitch of a note is determined by its position on the staff lines.

A SIGN CALLED A CLEF APPEARS AT THE BEGINNING OF EVERY STAFF. IT SHOWS THE PITCH THAT THE MUSIC SHOULD BE PLAYED AT. THERE ARE TWO MAIN TYPES OF CLEF:

| THE TREBLE CLEF | THE BASS CLEF |
|---|---|
| The treble clef (or "G" clef) is used when higher notes are being written down. | The bass clef (or "F" clef) is used when the lower notes are being represented. |

## ☆ WRITTEN NOTES

DIFFERENT LENGTHS OF NOTES HAVE DIFFERENT NAMES AND SYMBOLS. THEY GIVE MUSIC ITS RHYTHM. THIS TABLE LISTS THE MAIN TYPES OF NOTES AND HOW MANY BEATS THEY LAST FOR.

| NAME | SYMBOL | NUMBER OF BEATS |
|---|---|---|
| WHOLE NOTE (SEMIBREVE) | ○ | 4 |
| HALF NOTE (MINIM) | ♩ | 2 |
| QUARTER NOTE (CROTCHET) | ♩ | 1 |
| EIGHTH NOTE (QUAVER) | ♪ | ½ |
| SIXTEENTH NOTE (SEMIQUAVER) | ♬ | ¼ |

SO A WHOLE NOTE LASTS TWICE AS LONG AS A HALF NOTE, A HALF NOTE LASTS TWICE AS LONG AS A QUARTER NOTE, AND SO ON. THE NOTES ARE WRITTEN DOWN IN SMALL GROUPS, CALLED BARS. EACH BAR IS SEPARATED BY VERTICAL LINES.

# 13

## What other signs do we use?

## Look out for clues at the beginning of a piece of music.

**THE KEY SIGNATURE** This tells the musician which notes, if any, must be made sharp or flat so that a piece of music can be played in a particular scale.

SHARP ➤ # FLAT ➤ ♭

**THE TIME SIGNATURE** The top figure tells you the number of beats in a bar. The bottom one tells you the type of note which represents the beat.

3
4

Composers may also write signs or words above or below the staff lines to say how the music should be played, for example "pianissimo" (pp) = play very softly.

## Connect!

HOW DO COMPOSERS COMBINE NOTES TO MAKE US FEEL A CERTAIN WAY? CHECK OUT Q40.

## Connect!

DOES WRITTEN MUSIC ALWAYS LOOK LIKE THIS? FIND OUT IN Q53.

# 14

## Does everyone use these rules?

## No. Some musicians never write music down. Others use different notes and scales.

One reason Eastern music sounds different from Western music is because it uses different scales. If we count the notes represented by both black and white piano keys, a scale in Western music contains 12 notes in an octave. The Arab scale has 17 notes in an octave.

The basic Indian scale contains 7 notes, each with its own name—sa, re, ga, ma, pa, dha and ni. The notes represent certain moods:

**sa** and **ma** = peace
**re** = anger
**ga** and **dha** = seriousness
**pa** = joy **ni** = sadness

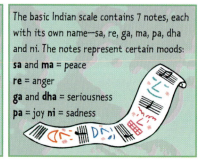

Exactly how is

# music

made?

What is the simplest instrument?

What's inside a guitar?

How did electricity change the sound of music?

You'll find the answers to these questions in
PART TWO of your musical journey.
Go on, turn the page! ---➤

QUESTION

# 15 How do we change a collection of sounds into music?

**Well, one way is to make instruments which create different kinds of sounds. These sounds can be organized into exciting and interesting patterns—in other words, music!**

## ☆ GROUPING INSTRUMENTS

There are many thousands of types of instruments around the world. Musical instruments create soundwaves by activating some part of their design. Xylophones have metal or wooden bars that vibrate when struck, guitars have nylon strings that are plucked, and clarinets have a reed—a thin piece of cane, wood or metal—around which air is breathed.

**ONE WAY OF GROUPING INSTRUMENTS TOGETHER IS TO LOOK AT THE WAY THEY PRODUCE SOUND.**

IDIOPHONES
MEMBRANOPHONES
AEROPHONES
CHORDOPHONES

## 1 Idiophones

Sound is produced by the vibration of the body of the instrument itself.

### Connect!

TURN TO Q42 TO SEE HOW BELLS ARE USED IN RELIGIOUS CEREMONIES IN CHINA.

### ☆ BELLS

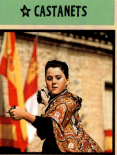

Bells range in size from small, delicate handbells to massive church bells weighing several tons. They are usually dome-shaped, made of metal and are hollow. Striking them with a hammer or clapper causes the whole instrument to vibrate and produce soundwaves.

### ☆ CASTANETS

Castanets are hollow pieces of wood held in the hand and used as clappers. In Spain, flamenco dancers produce a rhythm by clicking a pair rapidly together. They are naturally echoing, or resonant, because air inside the hollowed wood picks up the vibrations of the clicks and makes them louder.

### ☆ MUSICAL GLASSES

Musical glasses were popular in the 18th and 19th centuries. They produced sound in the same way as rubbing the rim of a wine glass. Both **JOSEPH HAYDN** (1732–1809) and **WOLFGANG AMADEUS MOZART** wrote music for them. The American president, Benjamin Franklin (1706–90), invented a version where the glasses turned and fitted inside each other. To sound a note, you simply touched the rim of the glass.

### Prove It!

Make your own set of musical glasses. Pour water into a wine glass (ask permission to use it first) and run a wet finger round the rim to make it sound. Now fill seven other glasses with less or more water to make a whole musical scale. Use the glasses to play simple tunes.

## ☆ GROUPING INSTRUMENTS IN CHINA

INSTRUMENTS ARE DIVIDED INTO EIGHT GROUPS, ACCORDING TO THE MATERIAL THEY ARE MADE OF:

| | |
|---|---|
| **METAL** (BELLS) | **SKIN** (DRUMS) |
| **STONE** (CHIMES) | **CLAY** (PIPES) |
| **SILK** (STRINGS) | **GOURD**—HOLLOW, DRIED |
| **BAMBOO** (FLUTES) | **VEGETABLE SUCH AS PUMPKIN** |
| **WOOD** (PERCUSSION INSTRUMENTS) | (WINDBOX FOR REED INSTRUMENTS) |

## Membranophones

Sound is produced by the vibration of a skin or membrane attached to a bowl, cylinder or frame.

### ☆ TIMPANI

Timpani, or kettledrums, are tuned drums, because they produce a definite note when struck. The pitch of the notes can be changed by tightening or loosening the skin covering the copper bowl.

## Prove It!

Put a comb next to your mouth and hum or speak into it. Then put a piece of tissue paper over the comb, and do the same again. Your voice now has a "buzz" to it. The "membrane" has changed the sound.

### ☆ TALKING DRUMS

These are found throughout West Africa. They have two membranes, which are held in place by leather cords stretching between them. Squeezing or relaxing the cords makes the pitch of the drum become higher or lower. The rhythms of the drums are often used as special codes to pass on messages.

### ☆ TABLA or TABLA-BANYA

These are a pair of small drums often used in Indian music. The tabla is struck with the right hand, and the banya with the left. Tabla players use their fingers to tap the centre of the skin and press down with their palms on the outer edge to vary the note.

## Aerophones

Sound is produced by the vibration of air caused by blowing into a hollow object.

### ☆ PIPES and FLUTES

These have a mouthpiece at one end and holes down the length of the column. Closing the holes, by placing the fingers on them, means air is trapped inside the pipe or flute. The pitch of a note depends on the length of the column of vibrating air inside.

**PICCOLO** 12 INCHES = PRODUCES HIGH NOTES.
**DOUBLE (CONTRA) BASSOON** ABOUT 16 FEET = PRODUCES LOW NOTES.

### ☆ CLARINET

The clarinet's mouthpiece contains a strip of cane, or plastic, called a reed. This shapes the sound as it vibrates against the mouthpiece when air is blown in. An early version was played by the Egyptians 3,000 years ago.

**Connect!** THE LARGEST INSTRUMENT EVER BUILT HAS THOUSANDS OF PIPES. SEE Q18.

### ☆ TRUMPETS

Trumpets are usually made of brass and have a cup-shaped mouthpiece. The pitch is controlled by a system of three valves.

☆ TRUMPETS, TROMBONES, TUBAS AND FRENCH HORNS ARE PART OF THE BRASS SECTION OF A WESTERN ORCHESTRA.

### ☆ CONCH HORN

This is made from a large shell. The tip of the shell is pierced and a small, wooden or bamboo mouthpiece is inserted into the hole. Blowing air into the shell produces a loud, cooing noise. The conch is played in Peru, Borneo, India and Portugal, often during religious ceremonies.

## Chordophones

Sound is produced by vibrating a string through plucking, hitting, rubbing, strumming, bowing or blowing it.

### ☆ SITAR

This instrument gives Indian music its distinctive shimmering sound. It has seven main strings, and beneath these lie between 11 and 19 extra strings known as sympathetic strings. Although the sympathetic strings are never played, they automatically vibrate when the main strings are plucked.

**Connect!** SOME INSTRUMENTS CREATE MUSICAL SOUND WITHOUT A HUMAN'S TOUCH. CHECK OUT Q20.

### ☆ VIOLIN

The four strings of a violin, or fiddle, are usually played by drawing a bow across them. One hand controls the bow, while the other hand chooses the notes to be played. Violins appeared in their present form in the 1500s. The first European fiddles, known as rebecs, were small and pear-shaped.

**Connect!** ONE PERSON BECAME VERY FAMOUS FOR MAKING THIS INSTRUMENT. SEE Q22.

### ☆ PIANO

When a key is pressed on the keyboard it operates a lever, which raises a small wooden hammer and makes it strike a string. In an upright piano, the steel strings are arranged vertically, while in a grand piano they are horizontal. The first piano was invented in about 1709 by **BARTOLOMMEO CHRISTOFORI** (1655-1731).

**Connect!** CHECK OUT Q24 TO SEE HOW ONE MUSICAL INSTRUMENT EVOLVES INTO ANOTHER.

☆ THE FLUTE AND CLARINET ARE PART OF THE WOODWIND SECTION OF A WESTERN ORCHESTRA.

☆ IN A WESTERN ORCHESTRA, PERCUSSION INSTRUMENTS ARE THOSE WHICH PRODUCE SOUND WHEN THEY ARE HIT, SHAKEN, CLICKED, RASPED OR SCRAPED. THEY ARE ALMOST ALL EITHER IDIOPHONES OR MEMBRANOPHONES.

## QUESTION

# 16  What is the oldest instrument?

Prehistoric people used natural objects, such as sticks, stones, bones, wood and shells, to make the first musical instruments.

### Connect!
WHICH INVENTION CHANGED THE KINDS OF INSTRUMENTS THAT COULD BE MADE? CHECK OUT Q29.

The oldest surviving instruments are mammoth bones from parts of northern Europe and Asia. The 35,000-year-old bones were banged together or blown to make music.

The tribes of South America made clay whistles shaped like birds, animals and people. Whistles made from the toe bones of reindeer have been found in the Dordogne region in France. They date from around 40,000 to 12,000 BC, and were probably used for signalling during reindeer hunts.

A musical note is produced when an arrow is released from a bow. This may have inspired the earliest stringed instruments. Harps and lyres were played more than 4,000 years ago by the people of Sumer (modern Iraq). Both have been found in the tombs of Sumerian kings and are pictured on ancient Egyptian wall paintings.

The vina is the oldest instrument played in India. In the Hindu religion, it is mentioned in a holy book more than 3,500 years old. The player plucks the seven main strings with long fingernails or a plectrum (small piece of metal). The wooden body is attached to two soundboxes made from gourds, which help to amplify the sound.

### Connect!
TURN TO Q27 TO SEE HOW TODAY'S MUSICIANS STILL MAKE INSTRUMENTS OUT OF WHATEVER MATERIALS ARE AVAILABLE.

---

## QUESTION

# 17  What is the most expensive instrument?

## The highest price ever paid for an instrument is $1,380,000.

This was the sum a 1720 Stradivarius violin sold for at auction in 1990.

**MOST EXPENSIVE GUITAR = $303,000**
A FENDER STRATOCASTER GUITAR BELONGING TO THE ROCK STAR JIMI HENDRIX WAS SOLD AT SOTHEBY'S, LONDON, IN 1990.

---

## QUESTION

# 18  What is the biggest instrument?

## Organs can fill an entire room.

The organ invented by the Greeks in 300 BC used water power to blow air through the pipes. Today electric fans are used. The pitch of the notes produced depends on the length and width of the pipes.

THE LARGEST INSTRUMENT EVER BUILT IS THE **AUDITORIUM ORGAN** IN ATLANTIC CITY, NEW JERSEY, USA. COMPLETED IN 1930, IT HAS 33,112 PIPES, RANGING IN HEIGHT FROM $^3/_{16}$ INCH TO 64 FEET. THESE ARE OPERATED BY 1,477 STOP CONTROLS.

---

## QUESTION

# 19  What are the simplest instruments?

## Probably percussion instruments.

Almost anything can be banged, scraped, shaken or beaten to make a musical sound.

A **BULLROARER** (OR **THUNDERSTICK**) IS A FLAT PIECE OF WOOD OR BONE, WHICH IS TIED TO A LONG STRING. WHEN SWUNG ROUND IN A CIRCLE IT MAKES A ROARING OR HUMMING SOUND. AMAZONIAN INDIANS USE THEM AS PROTECTION AGAINST EVIL SPIRITS.
**SCRAPERS** ARE MADE FROM WOODEN BLOCKS WITH GROOVES CUT INTO THE EDGES. THESE ARE RUBBED WITH ANOTHER STICK, PRODUCING A RASPING SOUND. THE PORTUGUESE RUB TOGETHER A COUPLE OF PINE CONES, WHILE AUSTRALIAN ABORIGINES OFTEN ACCOMPANY THEIR SONGS ON A NOTCHED STICK.

☆ WE USE OUR HANDS AS AN INSTRUMENT, WHEN WE CLAP, AND OUR VOICE, WHEN WE SING.

# 20 Can instruments make music without us?

## Yes. Some instruments have been designed to play "nature's music!"

Wind passing over a stretched string makes it vibrate. The length and thickness of the string and speed of the wind affect the sound.

### ☆ AEOLIAN HARPS

These were popular in central Europe in the 19th century. They are named after the Greek wind god, Aeolus. The harp consists of a shallow box 3 to 5 feet long with around 12 strings stretched along it. The strings are the same length, but differ in thickness. When the harp is left outside, the wind races through the strings and produces eerie sounds.

### Prove It!

Wind chimes are especially popular in Japan and China. They produce a soothing sound when the wind passes through them. Make and hang your own wind chimes, using blocks of wood, shells, pens, keys and bottles.

**Connect!** MUSICIANS ARE FASCINATED BY THE MUSIC OF NATURE. SEE Q28.

# 22 Does it make a difference who makes an instrument?

## Some instruments are considered valuable because they were made, or designed, by great craftsmen.

### ☆ STRADIVARI

The violin-maker **ANTONIO STRADIVARI** (1644–1737) worked in the town of Cremona, Italy. He made around a thousand violins and over 300 other stringed instruments, including violas, lutes and cellos. Stradivarius violins are thought to be the best. Half of his violins still exist and they fetch great prices when sold at auctions.

### ☆ LES PAUL

The American guitarist **LES PAUL** (born in 1915) invented the first solid body electric guitar in the early 1940s. In 1952, he designed a classic electric guitar for the Gibson company. The instrument was a model for many designs of electric guitar to come, and is one of the most widely used rock guitars in the world today.

# 21 How have some people changed the way instruments are played?

## Musicians may use traditional instruments to create new and unusual sounds.

**1** In a piece of music, the term pizzicato (Italian for "pinched") means the player should play a bowed stringed instrument by plucking the strings with the fingers. This technique was invented in the 17th century by the Italian composer **CLAUDIO MONTEVERDI** (1567–1643).

**2** The American composer **HENRY COWELL** (1897–1965) experimented with new ways of playing the piano. In *Aeolian Harp* (1923) he strummed the strings directly rather than using the keyboard. Two years later, in *The Banshee*, he created "note clusters" by pressing groups of keys down with a ruler.

**3** **JIMI HENDRIX** (1942–70) was famous for his daring and original style of playing the electric guitar, which included using his teeth.

**Connect!** HOW DO ELECTRIC GUITARS WORK AND DO THEY ALL LOOK THE SAME? SEE Q31.

# 23 Have people become famous for inventing instruments?

**Yes!**

The modern clarinet was invented around the beginning of the 18th century by **JOHANN DENNER**, a German instrument-maker.

The German instrument-maker **THEOBALD BOEHM** (1793–1881) invented hole coverings, or keys, for the flute. Today, flutes are still made in the same way.

The Belgian inventor **ADOLPHE SAX** created the saxophone about 1840, by enlarging the clarinet and building it from brass to make it louder. It was first used in military bands.

# 24 How does one instrument develop into another?

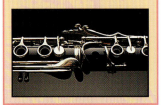

**LET'S TAKE A LOOK AT STRINGED INSTRUMENTS**

Since the first instruments were created, musicians have adapted designs and playing techniques in the search for new sounds. Each culture has its own musical traditions.

## ☆ ZITHER

Ground zithers, made in central Africa and southeast Asia, involve digging a hole in the ground and stretching a string across it. Plucking the string makes the air in the hole vibrate, producing musical notes. Zithers made from flat boxes developed in Austria and Bavaria in the 19th century. They had up to 45 strings, each tuned to a different pitch.

## ☆ KOTO

The koto is the traditional Japanese zither, which is about two

metres long. It rests on the floor and is played with both hands. Players pluck the 13 strings with ivory plectra worn on the thumb, index and middle fingers of the right hand. Underneath each string is a piece of wood, called a bridge. These are slid up and down to change the string's pitch.

## ☆ HARP

The first Egyptian harps, made over 4,000 years ago, probably evolved from the musical bow, which developed out of the archer's bow.

The concert harp has 47 strings of different lengths and pitches, tuned to a scale of notes. There are seven pedals which can be pressed to alter the pitch of the strings. This kind of harp is known as a frame harp.

## ☆ LUTE

The first lutes were made almost 4,000 years ago. Although popular in

Europe in the 17th and 18th centuries, the instrument's 26 strings meant it was difficult to play. So, by the end of the 18th century its popularity had faded. The traditional lute has a short neck attached to a hollow, pear-shaped body. This design influenced the look of the guitar and the violin.

# 25 How do you make a violin?

## The best violins are made by hand from carefully chosen materials.

**NICCOLO PAGANINI**
(1782–1840)
**ITALIAN VIOLINIST AND COMPOSER**
HE GAVE HIS FIRST PUBLIC PERFORMANCE WHEN HE WAS ONLY 12 YEARS OLD. SO FRENZIED AND BRILLIANT WAS HIS TECHNIQUE, THAT MANY PEOPLE BELIEVED HE HAD BEEN TAUGHT BY THE DEVIL HIMSELF.

**1**
**THE BODY IS CARVED.**
THE FRONT, OR "BELLY," OF THE VIOLIN IS MADE FROM SOFTWOOD, SUCH AS SPRUCE OR PINE. THE BACK IS MADE FROM HARDWOOD, USUALLY MAPLE. TEMPLATES ARE USED TO DRAW ONTO THE WOOD THE 70 OR SO SHAPES WHICH MAKE UP THE INSTRUMENT. AFTER BEING CUT OUT WITH A FINE SAW, THE WOOD IS CARVED ROUGHLY WITH A HOLLOW TOOL CALLED A GOUGE. IT IS THEN SMOOTHED OVER WITH A PLANE.

**2**
**FURTHER DETAILS ARE ADDED.**
A SMALL GROOVE IS CUT AROUND THE EDGE OF THE BELLY. THIS IS FILLED WITH A THIN STRIP OF FLEXIBLE WOOD CALLED THE PURFLING, WHICH STOPS THE WOOD FROM CRACKING. THE BELLY AND BACK ARE SHAPED—THE BELLY HAS AN EVEN THICKNESS OF AROUND $1/8$ INCH, THE BACK IS SLIGHTLY THICKER IN THE CENTER. THIS GIVES THE INSTRUMENT GREATER RESONANCE.

**3**
**FITTING THE RIBS.**
THE THIN SIDES, OR RIBS, OF THE VIOLIN ARE MADE FROM WOOD SUCH AS MAPLE. THEY ARE HEATED TO MAKE THEM FLEXIBLE, THEN SHAPED AROUND A WOODEN MOLD, WHICH CONTAINS SEVERAL WOODEN BLOCKS. THE RIBS ARE GLUED TO THESE, GIVING THEM SUPPORT AND KEEPING THEM IN ONE PIECE. THEY ALSO HELP TO FIX THE RIBS TO THE BODY OF THE VIOLIN WHEN EVERYTHING IS GLUED IN PLACE.

**4**
**THE FINISHING TOUCHES.**
F-SHAPED SOUNDHOLES ARE CUT IN THE BELLY. THE RIBS ARE ATTACHED TO THE BACK AND BELLY. THE NECK IS ADDED. THE LAYERS OF REDDISH-BROWN VARNISH APPLIED AFFECT THE SOUND OF THE INSTRUMENT. THE FINGERBOARD IS ADDED. THEN THE BRIDGE AND SOUNDPOST UNDERNEATH, WHICH HELP TO CARRY THE VIBRATIONS OF THE STRINGS THROUGHOUT THE INSTRUMENT. THE LAST STEP IS FITTING THE STRINGS.

# 26 What's inside an acoustic guitar?

## A soundboard and struts.

The **SOUNDBOARD** is the upper part of the body underneath the strings. It is normally made from wood such as pine, spruce and redwood. Of all the guitar's sections, the soundboard has the greatest influence on the quality of notes produced.

The soundboard is strengthened by having a pattern of wooden **STRUTS** glued on, making it strong enough to resist the tension of the strings. The pattern of struts helps to create the tone of the guitar.

### Prove It!

Loop elastic bands of various thicknesses around a tin. When you pluck the bands, the air in the tin will make the vibrations louder.

☆ THE DESIGN OF THE ACOUSTIC GUITAR WAS PERFECTED BY THE SPANISH GUITAR MAKER **ANTONIO DE TORRES JURADO.**

---

**Connect!** HOW DO CHANGING STYLES OF INSTRUMENTS REFLECT A CHANGING WORLD? SEE Q31.

**Connect!** HOW DID ELECTRICITY CHANGE THE SOUNDS THAT INSTRUMENTS COULD MAKE? SEE Q29.

### ☆ OUD, BALALAIKA, SHAMISEN

The oud is mainly played in Arab countries such as Egypt and Iraq. The main difference between the oud and European lutes is that it has two extra soundholes beneath the main, large one. Russian musicians play the balalaika, a flat, triangular-shaped lute. The Japanese shamisen is a long-necked lute with three strings running over a square body, covered with catskin or dogskin.

### ☆ SPIKE FIDDLE, REBEC, REBAB

The Middle Eastern spike fiddle, made around the 10th century, was the first bowed fiddle. It had a wooden or iron spike running through it, which rested on the floor. The three strings were bowed. The earliest European fiddle, played in the Middle Ages, was the small, pear-shaped rebec, which evolved from the Arabian rebab.

### ☆ VIOLIN, CELLO, DOUBLE BASS

The violin appeared in the middle of the 16th century. It is tucked into the neck, and a horsehair bow is drawn across the four strings to make them sound. The larger cello (or violoncello) has four strings, tuned an octave lower than the viola. The double bass, at almost two metres tall, is played standing up. The electric bass guitar has a similar range.

### ☆ GUITAR

The classic figure-eight body with its six strings dates back to the mid-19th century. The first Spanish guitars arrived from North Africa, and probably descended from the oud. Electric guitars became popular in the 1950s. Unlike the acoustic guitar, the electric guitar often has a solid, compact body.

QUESTION

# 27

## How have people used whatever is available to make musical instruments?

**Instruments have traditionally been made from natural materials such as bone, wood and stone. With skill and imagination, most objects can be used to create music.**

The **MOLO** is a simple Nigerian lute. Its soundbox is sometimes made from an old sardine can.

The **MBILA**, from Mozambique, southeast Africa, is a wooden xylophone with a row of gourds underneath. Each contains a hole covered over with a spider's egg case, which produces a buzzing sound when the bars are struck.

In the African **SANSA**, metal tongues attached to a wooden base are played by twanging with the thumbs. The tongues are often made of scrap metal from bicycle spokes, umbrella ribs, car springs and old saw blades. The European musical box is a mechanical version of the sansa.

### ☆ CARIBBEAN STEEL BANDS

The steel bands of the Caribbean use large oil drums as their main instrument. To make a steel pan, the top of the oil drum is heated and hammered to create different sunken sections. Each section sounds a different note when struck with a pair of rubber-tipped beaters.

| HIGHEST ·········· ➔ DEEPEST | | | |
|---|---|---|---|
| PING PONG | GUITAR PAN | CELLOPAN | BOOM |

### ☆ NORTH AMERICAN INDIAN FLUTES

North American Indians split tree branches in half lengthways and hollow them out. They are then stuck back together again with a glue made from boiled animal skin scrapings, and tied tight with rawhide strips. In the past, men played the flutes to woo female members of the tribe.

IN THE 19TH CENTURY, A LONDON STONEMASON CALLED **JOSEPH RICHARDSON** BUILT THE **ROCK HARMONICON**—A MASSIVE XYLOPHONE WITH BARS MADE OF ROCK. THE INSTRUMENT TOOK 13 YEARS TO CONSTRUCT. IT WAS PLAYED WITH MALLETS.

**Prove It!**

Make a simple rattle by shaking seeds, beans, beads and anything else you can find, in a container.

**Connect!** HOW DO MUSICIANS "SAMPLE" EVERYDAY NOISES? SEE Q30.

QUESTION

# 28

## Are musicians influenced by the sound of nature?

### Yes.

Early music was inspired by the sound of the wind, water and birdsong. Today, musicians still look to the natural world for inspiration.

In his *Toy Symphony*, **JOSEPH HAYDN** used the chirrups of a water whistle to suggest the singing of a nightingale.

**OLIVIER MESSIAEN** (1908–92) collected examples of birdsong from all over France, scribbling them down in musical notation. He used this music in many of his pieces, including the 1935 piano and orchestra work *Reveil des Oiseaux* (The Waking of the Birds).

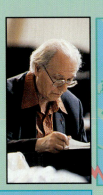

Some musicians combine the actual sounds produced by animals with their own compositions. In *Out of the Depths*, **TERRY OLDFIELD** accompanies flute melodies and female vocals with whale songs. **MEDWYN GOODALL**'s *Way of the Dolphin* features the underwater songs of dolphins. The howling of wolves adds a mystical quality on *Even Wolves Dream* by the composer **ANTHONY MILES**.

**Connect!** TURN TO Q46 TO FIND OUT HOW THIS COMPOSER USED MUSIC TO GET HIS OPINION ACROSS TO A PRINCE.

**Connect!** THIS COMPOSER EXPERIMENTED WITH ONE OF THE FIRST ELECTRONIC INSTRUMENTS. FIND OUT MORE IN Q29.

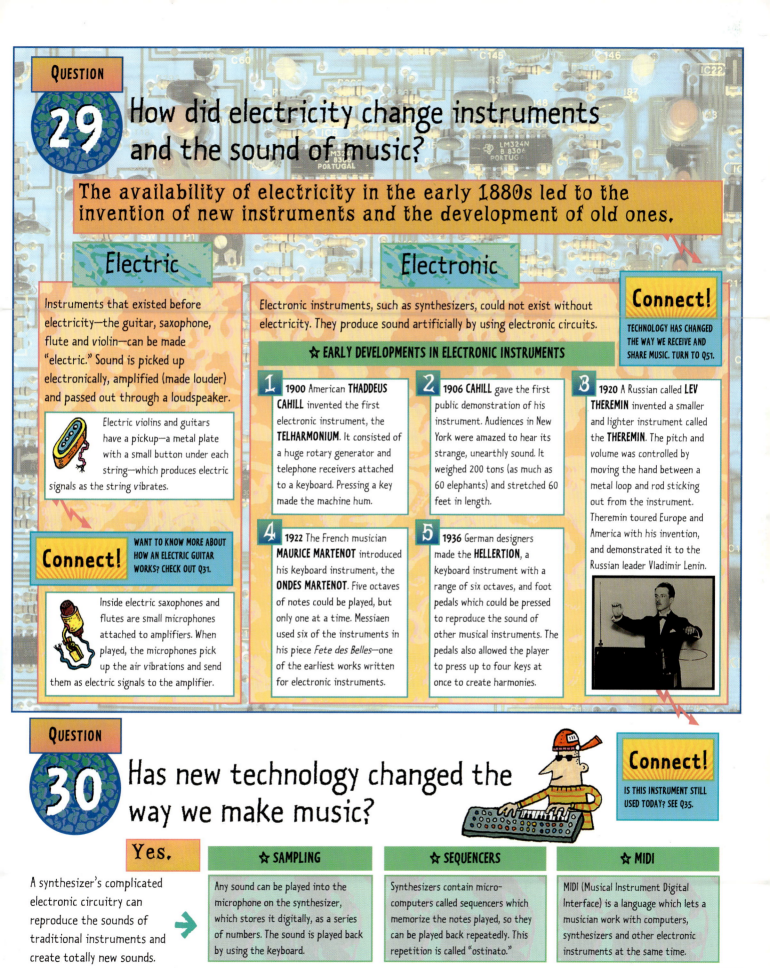

# 29

# How did electricity change instruments and the sound of music?

**The availability of electricity in the early 1880s led to the invention of new instruments and the development of old ones.**

## Electric

Instruments that existed before electricity—the guitar, saxophone, flute and violin—can be made "electric." Sound is picked up electronically, amplified (made louder) and passed out through a loudspeaker.

Electric violins and guitars have a pickup—a metal plate with a small button under each string—which produces electric signals as the string vibrates.

**Connect!** WANT TO KNOW MORE ABOUT HOW AN ELECTRIC GUITAR WORKS? CHECK OUT Q31.

Inside electric saxophones and flutes are small microphones attached to amplifiers. When played, the microphones pick up the air vibrations and send them as electric signals to the amplifier.

## Electronic

Electronic instruments, such as synthesizers, could not exist without electricity. They produce sound artificially by using electronic circuits.

### ☆ EARLY DEVELOPMENTS IN ELECTRONIC INSTRUMENTS

**1** 1900 American **THADDEUS CAHILL** invented the first electronic instrument, the **TELHARMONIUM**. It consisted of a huge rotary generator and telephone receivers attached to a keyboard. Pressing a key made the machine hum.

**2** 1906 **CAHILL** gave the first public demonstration of his instrument. Audiences in New York were amazed to hear its strange, unearthly sound. It weighed 200 tons (as much as 60 elephants) and stretched 60 feet in length.

**3** 1920 A Russian called **LEV THEREMIN** invented a smaller and lighter instrument called the **THEREMIN**. The pitch and volume was controlled by moving the hand between a metal loop and rod sticking out from the instrument. Theremin toured Europe and America with his invention, and demonstrated it to the Russian leader Vladimir Lenin.

**4** 1922 The French musician **MAURICE MARTENOT** introduced his keyboard instrument, the **ONDES MARTENOT**. Five octaves of notes could be played, but only one at a time. Messiaen used six of the instruments in his piece *Fete des Belles*—one of the earliest works written for electronic instruments.

**5** 1936 German designers made the **HELLERTION**, a keyboard instrument with a range of six octaves, and foot pedals which could be pressed to reproduce the sound of other musical instruments. The pedals also allowed the player to press up to four keys at once to create harmonies.

**Connect!** TECHNOLOGY HAS CHANGED THE WAY WE RECEIVE AND SHARE MUSIC. TURN TO Q51.

# 30

# Has new technology changed the way we make music?

**Connect!** IS THIS INSTRUMENT STILL USED TODAY? SEE Q35.

## Yes.

A synthesizer's complicated electronic circuitry can reproduce the sounds of traditional instruments and create totally new sounds.

### ☆ SAMPLING

Any sound can be played into the microphone on the synthesizer, which stores it digitally, as a series of numbers. The sound is played back by using the keyboard.

### ☆ SEQUENCERS

Synthesizers contain micro-computers called sequencers which memorize the notes played, so they can be played back repeatedly. This repetition is called "ostinato."

### ☆ MIDI

MIDI (Musical Instrument Digital Interface) is a language which lets a musician work with computers, synthesizers and other electronic instruments at the same time.

# 31

## How do changing styles of instruments reflect the changing world?

As audiences grew bigger, people wanted to hear music played louder, more flamboyantly and on new, dynamic instruments. The electric guitar was invented because the acoustic guitar could not be heard by large groups of people.

**Connect!**

HOW DO TODAY'S POP CONCERTS DIFFER FROM THE FIRST CONCERTS HELD? TURN TO Q51.

☆ **THE ELECTRIC GUITAR—ADAPTED FOR A CHANGING WORLD...**

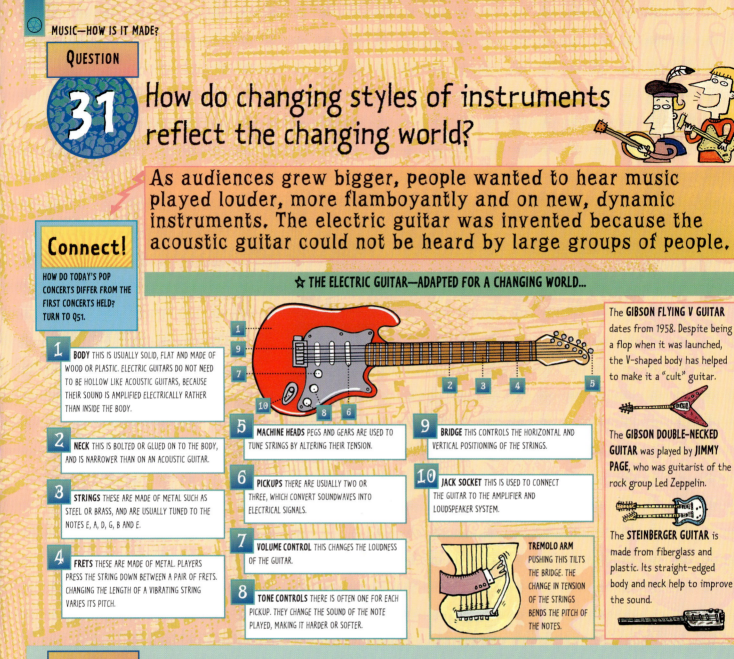

**1** BODY THIS IS USUALLY SOLID, FLAT AND MADE OF WOOD OR PLASTIC. ELECTRIC GUITARS DO NOT NEED TO BE HOLLOW LIKE ACOUSTIC GUITARS, BECAUSE THEIR SOUND IS AMPLIFIED ELECTRICALLY RATHER THAN INSIDE THE BODY.

**2** NECK THIS IS BOLTED OR GLUED ON TO THE BODY, AND IS NARROWER THAN ON AN ACOUSTIC GUITAR.

**3** STRINGS THESE ARE MADE OF METAL SUCH AS STEEL OR BRASS, AND ARE USUALLY TUNED TO THE NOTES E, A, D, G, B AND E.

**4** FRETS THESE ARE MADE OF METAL. PLAYERS PRESS THE STRING DOWN BETWEEN A PAIR OF FRETS. CHANGING THE LENGTH OF A VIBRATING STRING VARIES ITS PITCH.

**5** MACHINE HEADS PEGS AND GEARS ARE USED TO TUNE STRINGS BY ALTERING THEIR TENSION.

**6** PICKUPS THERE ARE USUALLY TWO OR THREE, WHICH CONVERT SOUNDWAVES INTO ELECTRICAL SIGNALS.

**7** VOLUME CONTROL THIS CHANGES THE LOUDNESS OF THE GUITAR.

**8** TONE CONTROLS THERE IS OFTEN ONE FOR EACH PICKUP. THEY CHANGE THE SOUND OF THE NOTE PLAYED, MAKING IT HARDER OR SOFTER.

**9** BRIDGE THIS CONTROLS THE HORIZONTAL AND VERTICAL POSITIONING OF THE STRINGS.

**10** JACK SOCKET THIS IS USED TO CONNECT THE GUITAR TO THE AMPLIFIER AND LOUDSPEAKER SYSTEM.

TREMOLO ARM PUSHING THIS TILTS THE BRIDGE. THE CHANGE IN TENSION OF THE STRINGS BENDS THE PITCH OF THE NOTES.

The **GIBSON FLYING V GUITAR** dates from 1958. Despite being a flop when it was launched, the V-shaped body has helped to make it a "cult" guitar.

The **GIBSON DOUBLE-NECKED GUITAR** was played by **JIMMY PAGE**, who was guitarist of the rock group Led Zeppelin.

The **STEINBERGER GUITAR** is made from fiberglass and plastic. Its straight-edged body and neck help to improve the sound.

# 32

## What is an orchestra?

An orchestra is an organized collection of musicians playing together as a group.

Classical orchestras originated in Europe in the 16th century. In 17th century France, orchestras were specially employed to play at the court of King Louis XIV. One way of demonstrating wealth was to employ more musicians, so the size of orchestras began to grow.

| END OF 18TH CENTURY | END OF 19TH CENTURY |
|---|---|
| ORCHESTRAS HAD AROUND 10 DIFFERENT INSTRUMENTS AND 50 PLAYERS. | ORCHESTRAS HAD AROUND 20 DIFFERENT INSTRUMENTS AND 100 PLAYERS. |

**Connect!**

SEE HOW SOME COMPOSERS HAVE USED UNUSUAL INSTRUMENTS IN AN ORCHESTRA IN Q53.

**WHAT'S IN A SYMPHONY ORCHESTRA?**

**STRINGS** = VIOLINS, VIOLAS, CELLOS AND DOUBLE BASSES.

**WOODWIND** = CLARINETS, FLUTES, OBOES AND BASSOONS.

**BRASS** = TRUMPETS, HORNS, TROMBONES AND TUBAS.

**PERCUSSION** = DRUMS, CYMBALS, TRIANGLES, XYLOPHONES, ETC.

☆ CONDUCTORS GUIDE THE ORCHESTRA'S MUSICIANS. IN THE 18TH CENTURY THE ROLE WAS TAKEN BY THE LEAD VIOLINIST, USING HIS BOW.

# 33

## What are the main types of Western classical music?

Classical composers invented various structures for their music, and then developed and adapted them.

| ☆ OPERA | ☆ ROMANTIC MUSIC | ☆ ORATORIO | ☆ SYMPHONY | ☆ CHAMBER MUSIC |
|---|---|---|---|---|
| **A MUSICAL DRAMA WHERE SINGING TAKES THE PLACE OF SPEECH.** Opera originated in late 16th century Florence, Italy, when a group of poets and musicians started setting Greek and Roman myths to music. Many classical musicians wrote opera scores, including **MOZART** (*The Magic Flute*), **BEETHOVEN** (*Fidelio*) and **BIZET** (*Carmen*). | **MUSIC WHICH EXPRESSES EMOTIONS OR SETS A SCENE.** In the 19th century composers started to write music that expressed their moods and feelings, or that told a story. They were inspired by nature. **CHOPIN, LISZT** and **SCHUMANN** wrote free-flowing piano pieces to try to capture their passion for the open air, forests and oceans. | **RELIGIOUS STORIES SET TO ORCHESTRAL MUSIC.** In the 17th century, composers began writing dramatic music based on Bible stories. Singers took the roles of the characters, and they were accompanied by a chorus and orchestra. Oratorios include *The Creation* by **HAYDN**, *Christmas Oratorio* by **BACH** and *Elijah* by **MENDELSSOHN**. | **ORCHESTRAL COMPOSITION WRITTEN IN THREE OR FOUR PARTS.** The separate parts of a symphony are called movements. The outside movements usually begin and end in a similar mood. The inside movements normally contrast, for example, one is slow and the next one is lively. **HAYDN** wrote 104 symphonies. | **MUSIC WRITTEN FOR A SMALL GROUP OF INSTRUMENTS.** In the 16th and 17th centuries wealthy families would gather in the evenings in a room, or chamber, and play music together. Gradually, classical musicians began writing chamber music for between two and eight instruments. A string quartet has two violins, a viola and a cello. |
| **NAME: RICHARD WAGNER** (1813–83) **NATIONALITY:** GERMAN WAGNER CHANGED THE FACE OF 19TH CENTURY OPERA. HIS VISION WAS OF A MUSICAL DRAMA WHICH COMBINED ALL THE ARTS—MUSIC, DANCE, POETRY AND SCENERY. HIS MOST FAMOUS WORK IS *DER RING DES NIBELUNGEN*—FOUR OPERAS WRITTEN OVER A PERIOD OF 21 YEARS. | **NAME: FELIX MENDELSSOHN** (1809–47) **NATIONALITY:** GERMAN MENDELSSOHN GAVE HIS FIRST PUBLIC CONCERT AT THE AGE OF NINE. HIS POPULAR ROMANTIC WORK CALLED *THE HEBRIDES OVERTURE* (1832), WAS INSPIRED BY THE RUGGED, WILD SCENERY OF THE SCOTTISH ISLANDS. | **NAME: GEORGE FRIDERIC HANDEL** (1685–1759) **NATIONALITY:** GERMAN HANDEL'S ORATORIOS WERE POPULAR BECAUSE OF THEIR BOLD CHORAL SINGING AND FAMILIAR STORYLINES. HIS MOST FAMOUS ORATORIO, *MESSIAH* (1742), TELLS THE STORY OF CHRIST. | **NAME: LUDWIG VAN BEETHOVEN** (1770–1827) **NATIONALITY:** GERMAN AT 26 BEETHOVEN BEGAN TO GO DEAF. HIS UNHAPPINESS GAVE RISE TO POWERFUL MUSIC, DEVELOPING THE FORM OF THE SYMPHONY. HIS *NINTH SYMPHONY* INTRODUCED SOLO VOICES. | **NAME: WOLFGANG AMADEUS MOZART** (1756–91) **NATIONALITY:** AUSTRIAN MOZART BEGAN COMPOSING MUSIC WHEN HE WAS FIVE. IN HIS SHORT LIFE HE WROTE OVER 600 PIECES OF MUSIC, INCLUDING 49 SYMPHONIES, 21 OPERAS AND 26 STRING QUARTETS. |

**Connect!** TURN TO Q48 TO SEE HOW MODERN MUSICIANS TELL STORIES ABOUT THEIR LIVES.

# 34

## Are there many famous women composers?

No, in the past women were not encouraged to write or play. Much of the contribution they did make was not recorded.

 Mozart's older sister, **MARIANNE**, was an accomplished pianist and composer. When they were young, their father took them both on a tour of European courts, where they entertained the nobility by playing solos and duets. Marianne became a teacher, but died in poverty in 1820.

 Schumann's wife, **CLARA**, was a talented pianist. Her father had been the famous composer's piano teacher. Although she did compose music, professional composition was not considered to be a woman's job. When she did perform in public, she often played her husband's work.

 **FANNY MENDELSSOHN** was the sister of Felix. They were both trained in music when they were children. Fanny would often advise her brother on his compositions, but rarely performed her own. On the one occasion that her family did allow her to play in public, she chose one of Felix's piano pieces.

QUESTION

# 35 How have composers been influenced by music from the past?

Composers and musicians may take traditional musical forms, instruments and sounds, and play with them to create a new and innovative style of music. This is how musical styles develop.

**Connect!**

TURN TO Q53 TO SEE HOW BREAKING THE RULES OF CLASSICAL MUSIC CAN SHOCK THE AUDIENCE.

## ☆ STOCKHAUSEN

In 1955–56, the German composer **KARLHEINZ STOCKHAUSEN** (born in 1928) experimented with traditional songwriting. He used recordings of a boy singing and speaking and then played with the sound, speeding it up, slowing it down and playing it backwards. This is called "musique concrète." The piece was called *Song of the Young Boy*.

## ☆ THE BEACH BOYS

Musicians may decide to put together unusual combinations of instruments to create an interesting effect. The 1960s American pop group **THE BEACH BOYS** produced an unusual record in 1966 called *Good Vibrations*. They used the unearthly sounds of the theremin.

**Connect!**

WHY DO SOME PEOPLE BECOME LEGENDS? CHECK OUT Q54.

QUESTION

# 36 Are composers inspired by music from other cultures?

### Yes!

COMPOSERS HAVE BEEN INFLUENCED BY MUSIC WHICH FOLLOWS TRADITIONS AND RULES OUTSIDE THEIR OWN EXPERIENCES.

The Indian composer **A R REHMAN**'s music for films, for example *Rangeela* (1995), blends Western rhythms and instruments with traditional Indian sounds and vocals.

The Japanese musician **TORU TAKEMITSU** (born 1930) combines a traditional Japanese gagaku orchestra with a Western symphony orchestra in his compositions *November Steps* and *Asterism*.

In 1968, Rolling Stones guitarist **BRIAN JONES** (1942–69) travelled to Jojouka, a village in Morocco. He recorded the exotic sounds played by local musicians on their flutes, drums and oboe-like instruments called rhaitas.

The American composer **STEVE REICH** (born 1936) is inspired by the music of Indonesia and Africa. Gamelan orchestras and African drums often repeat a series of notes or a rhythm pattern over and over again. Reich uses these effects in his own work.

The British group **THE BEATLES** also experimented with different instruments and sounds. In 1965 they used a sitar—an Indian stringed instrument—on their song *Norwegian Wood*. They were inspired by their developing interest in India.

**Connect!**

AS MUSICAL TRADITIONS AND IDEAS SPREAD AROUND THE WORLD, WHAT WILL HAPPEN TO MUSIC? SEE Q55.

QUESTION

# 37 What is improvised music?

Music that changes depending on the feelings of the player or on some other chance element.

● JAZZ MUSIC WAS FIRST PLAYED IN THE EARLY 1900s IN NEW ORLEANS, LOUISIANA, USA. ONE MUSICIAN PLAYS A TUNE AND DEVELOPS IT. THE REST JOIN IN, ADDING TO THE THEME.
● **JOHN CAGE** (1912–1992) CREATED *IMAGINARY LANDSCAPE NO 4* FOR 12 RADIOS, WHICH PICK UP DIFFERENT STATIONS EACH TIME THE PIECE IS PERFORMED.
● AFRICAN AND ASIAN MUSIC IS RARELY WRITTEN DOWN. THIS MEANS THAT NO PIECE OF MUSIC IS EVER PLAYED IN THE SAME WAY TWICE.

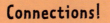

How does music make us

# feel

and why does it move us?

Have we always danced to music?

How does music tell us what is going on in the world?

## Can music shock?

The answers to all these questions will be answered in the final part of your journey. Turn the page and read PART THREE. ---->

# 38 Is music magic?

(HOW DOES IT MAKE US FEEL AND BEHAVE?)

MUSIC HAS BEEN ASSOCIATED WITH MAGIC FOR CENTURIES...

**Music can have an amazing effect on our emotions. It makes us cry and feel joy or pain. It can also remind us of past experiences.**

SCIENTISTS BELIEVE THAT PLAYING MUSIC TO A BABY IN THE WOMB CAN STIMULATE OR RELAX IT. MUSIC MAY HELP THE UNBORN BABY IMPROVE ITS BRAIN ACTIVITY AND LEARNING ABILITIES.

## ☆ ORPHEUS

In Greek myths, Orpheus was a musician who sang and played the lyre beautifully. When his wife, Eurydice, died from a snake bite, he tried to bring her back by performing in front of Hades, the king of the underworld. So delighted was Hades with the music, that he agreed to let Orpheus lead his wife back to the land of the living—but only if he didn't gaze back at her during their journey. Unfortunately, Orpheus couldn't resist stealing a look, and Eurydice was lost forever.

## ☆ PAN

The ancient Greek god Pan was in love with a young girl. But she did not love him back, so she ran away from him. Realizing how frightened she was, the other gods changed her into a reed for protection. Pan was so upset that he cut the reed into pipes of different lengths to make an instrument. He played haunting music on the panpipes to mourn the girl he had loved so dearly and then lost.

## ☆ SNAKE CHARMERS

In India and Pakistan, some musicians play a type of double clarinet called a tiktiri to charm snakes. The snakes appear to sway in time to the hypnotic music. In fact, snakes have very poor hearing. They cannot sense soundwaves, and usually rely on vibrations in the ground. So the charmed snakes are not responding to the music, but to the swinging movements of the charmer's pipe.

**Connect!** SOMETIMES PEOPLE ARE TRANSFIXED BY THE POWER OF MUSIC. SEE Q

# 39 Why do we all respond differently to music?

**Some people believe that we do not just hear music—we "perceive" it as well.**

MUSIC IS PLAYED → YOU HEAR MUSIC → YOU REACT ACCORDING TO...

Perceiving music means that we relate to it with our minds and other senses, as well as hearing the sounds made. Each person in an audience has different past experiences. Their feelings and moods as they listen to the music are also unique.

☆ YOUR EXPERIENCE
YOU THINK I HEAR MUSIC, SOUND, NOISE = YOU FEEL INTERESTED
YOU THINK IT REMINDS ME OF LAST SUMMER = YOU FEEL HAPPY
YOU THINK IT REMINDS ME OF THE BEST FRIEND I NEVER SEE = YOU FEEL SAD

☆ YOUR MOOD
YOU THINK I'M TIRED AND STRESSED = YOU FEEL IRRITABLE
YOU THINK I FEEL ENERGETIC AND WANT TO DANCE = YOU FEEL JOYOUS
YOU THINK I'M HAPPY BEING HERE = YOU FEEL COMFORTABLE

☆ THE MOMENT
YOU THINK THIS IS BETTER THAN BEING AT HOME = YOU FEEL POSITIVE
YOU THINK I CAN SMELL SOME LOVELY FLOWERS = YOU FEEL RELAXED
YOU THINK I CAN HEAR SOMEONE LAUGH = YOU FEEL CONTENT

OUR PERCEPTION BRINGS TOGETHER ALL THESE ELEMENTS, COMBINING THEM TO CREATE A STATE OF MIND. THIS DETERMINES HOW WE FEEL ABOUT THE MUSIC.

# 40

## What techniques do musicians use to affect our emotions?

When you next watch television listen carefully to the music. How does it make you feel? Now turn down the volume. Does it make a difference?

Composers may deliberately select specific arrangements of notes, whose combinations conjure up different moods in the listener.

**1 SCALES, NOTES AND MOOD** In Western music, the notes in major or minor scales rise or fall in pitch according to a sequence of intervals (distance between two notes). Intervals consist of either tones or semitones. Because of the positioning of the tones and semitones, melodies written in a major scale usually sound happy. Those based on a minor scale are often sad. A composer may raise the pitch of a note—the note becomes "sharp"— or lower the pitch—the note becomes "flat." This is another way of creating mood in music.

**2 RHYTHM AND MOOD** Rhythm helps give music character. Music from Latin America often uses fast, lively rhythms, featuring many drums and percussion instruments. This gives the music a driving beat. Sometimes, composers upset a regular beat by emphasizing beats of the bar which are not normally stressed. This is called "syncopation," and is used in jazz and West Indian calypso songs.

**4 HARMONY AND MOOD** Harmony is created when two or more notes are sounded together. Experimenting with different types of harmony can affect our moods.
**CONSONANT HARMONY** = SOUNDS SMOOTH AND PLEASANT.
**DISSONANT HARMONY** = SOUNDS ROUGH AND TENSE.

**RAGAS** THE NOTES ON AN INDIAN SCALE ARE ARRANGED IN PATTERNS CALLED RAGAS. EACH RAGA HAS A SPECIAL MEANING, AND COMBINATIONS MAY BE USED TO INFLUENCE THE LISTENER'S MOODS. SOME RAGAS ARE ASSOCIATED WITH THE TIME OF DAY (SUNRISE, NOON, DUSK) OR SEASON (SPRING, SUMMER, AUTUMN).

**3 TONE AND MOOD** The choice of instrument and the quality of its musical sound (called tone, or timbre) also determine the way music affects the audience. Different instruments have different tones depending on how they are made and how they produce sound. Flutes have a smooth, bright sound, while oboes are more nasal. Composers combine tones to create a piece of music in the same way that an artist mixes and arranges colours to create a picture.

☆ FILMS USE MUSIC TO GOOD EFFECT. AUDIENCES CAN BE SOOTHED WITH A GENTLE, REPEATED MELODY, OR SHOCKED WITH A SUDDEN CRASH OF CHORDS.

**Connect!** WHAT HAPPENS WHEN COMPOSERS CREATE WHOLE NEW COMBINATIONS OF TONES AND SEMITONES? SEE Q53.

# 41

## Why do we remember some melodies and not others?

A piece of music may be significant to us—it may remind us of good or bad times. Melodies may also follow set patterns.

Pop songs are often written with a catchy chorus or phrase, called a "hook," which draws the listener in. The hook is usually easy to hum and remember.

**A SONG MAY CONSIST OF:**
● MELODY 1 (repeated twice), followed by MELODY 2, then back to MELODY 1.
● MELODY 1, followed by MELODY 2—and then the whole sequence repeated.

**Connect!** SOME MUSICIANS PRODUCE MELODIES AND LYRICS THAT ARE SO POPULAR THEY BECOME MILLIONAIRES! CHECK OUT Q54.

QUESTION

# 42 How is music linked to religion?

**For thousands of years, music has been used to call people to prayer and as part of the religious ceremony itself.**

### ☆ INDIA

Classical Indian music developed over 2,000 years ago, as part of Hindu festivals and celebrations. The shahnai is a double-reeded oboe-like instrument, which has been played for many centuries in temples and mosques.

### ☆ TIBET

As part of their religious ceremonies, monks in Tibetan monasteries blow large horns. They also beat hanging drums. The music creates a holy atmosphere which helps the monks to focus their prayers and meditate (exercise their minds spiritually).

### ☆ PAKISTAN

Religious songs, called qawwalis, are sung in praise of Allah, the Muslim name for God. Musicians play the tabla, large tong cymbals and the Indian harmonium (powered by air from a hand-operated set of bellows attached to the instrument).

### ☆ CHINA

Bells are found in almost all Chinese temples. They do not usually have a clapper, but are struck with beaters. On New Year's Eve, every temple strikes its bells to see in the New Year. One of the oldest bells in the world comes from China. It is struck with a wooden beam, which is moved like a battering ram.

### ☆ EUROPE

Before the 18th century, most musicians worked either for the church or royalty. The composer **JOHANN SEBASTIAN BACH** (1685-1750) was employed at St Thomas's Church and school in Leipzig, Germany. He composed music for church services, trained the choir and taught music in the school.

### ☆ USA

In the 19th century, black slaves in the southern states of America sang "spirituals." They adapted Biblical stories to explain how they felt, as they spent long hours laboring on the cotton plantations. One worker sang a line and the others sang one back in response. This "call and response" is still heard in black churches and gospel choirs.

### Connect!

HOW DO MUSICIANS TELL THE STORIES OF THEIR LIVES TODAY? SEE Q48.

---

QUESTION

# 43 How is music linked to war?

**The drumming and trumpeting helped to boost morale, and were also used to pass on signals.**

### ☆ JERICHO

Jericho was a walled town in Jordan, in the Middle East. It was conquered in the 13th century BC by the Jews, who were led by Joshua. According to the Bible, the walls came tumbling down to the blast of the trumpets played by Joshua and his army.

### ☆ TRUMPETS

Trumpets helped soldiers in the armies of ancient Greece and Rome march to a steady beat. On the battlefield a trumpet blast would tell the soldiers when to attack or retreat.

### ☆ MILITARY BANDS

Since the late 18th century, military bands with portable brass instruments, such as trumpets and tubas, have been popular. Bagpipes are also used all over the world. The player blows air into a bag held under the arm. The air is squeezed by the arm through the pipes. As it is forced out, the air makes the reeds inside the pipes vibrate, creating a wailing sound.

# 44 Can music heal?

Music's rhythms and harmonies have a powerful impact on our senses. Music can make us feel happier and at peace with ourselves.

ON THE NORTHWEST PACIFIC COAST OF AMERICA, A SHAMAN USES A SPECIAL RATTLE MADE FROM A GOURD AND FILLED WITH BONES OR SEEDS, TO CURE THE SICK. THE INSTRUMENT IS THOUGHT TO HAVE HEALING PROPERTIES.

MEDITATION IS THE ART OF PHYSICALLY AND MENTALLY RELAXING THE BODY. MUSIC AND CHANTING CAN BE USED TO CREATE A CALMING ATMOSPHERE AND TO GIVE THE INDIVIDUAL A FOCUS.

IN HOSPITALS, PATIENTS WORKING WITH A TRAINED MUSIC THERAPIST ARE ENCOURAGED TO MAKE MUSIC. THIS OFTEN BUILDS CONFIDENCE AND RELAXES THEM, HELPING THEM TO REVEAL DEEP FEELINGS TO THE THERAPIST.

# 45 How do musicians describe love?

For centuries, love has been a constant theme in classical and popular music.

**THE ROMANTIC COMPOSERS**
The Romantic composers of the 19th century used music to express emotions and moods and describe themes of freedom and passion. In his *Symphonie Fantastique* (1830), the French composer **HECTOR BERLIOZ** (1803–69) painted a musical picture of his mad, undying love for an actress.

**MUSICALS**
Musicals based on themes of love have been highly successful. *Phantom of the Opera* (1986), by **ANDREW LLOYD WEBBER** (born 1948), is based on the novel by Gaston Leroux and tells of the doomed love between Christine, an opera singer, and the phantom of the Paris Opera House.

**"POP" SONGS**
Popular songs often deal with love and feelings. Many of **THE BEATLES'** most famous songs are about love, including *Love Me Do* (1962), *She Loves You* (1963), *I Want to Hold Your Hand* (1964) and *Can't Buy Me Love* (1964).

# 46 How have people used music to have their say?

Musicians can influence politicians and people generally by carefully selecting the style and content of their music.

### ☆ BEETHOVEN

BEETHOVEN WAS GREATLY INFLUENCED BY THE FRENCH REVOLUTION IN 1789. HE THOUGHT NAPOLEON BONAPARTE WAS A HERO FOR TAKING CONTROL OF THE COUNTRY BY OVERTHROWING THE KING, AND CALLED HIS THIRD SYMPHONY *BONAPARTE*. IN 1804, BEETHOVEN DID NOT AGREE WITH NAPOLEON DECLARING HIMSELF EMPEROR OF FRANCE, SO HE RETITLED HIS SYMPHONY *EROICA* ('HEROIC').

### ☆ HAYDN

HAYDN'S *FAREWELL SYMPHONY* (1772) WAS HIS WAY OF TELLING HIS EMPLOYER, PRINCE ESTERHAZY OF VIENNA, THAT HE NEEDED A HOLIDAY. THE PRINCE, WHO HAD SUDDENLY CANCELLED THE ORCHESTRA'S SUMMER BREAK, HEARD THE PIECE AND TOOK THE HINT. THE MUSICIANS GOT THEIR HOLIDAY BACK!

### ☆ "PROTEST MUSIC"

FOLK-ROCK MUSICIANS OF THE 1960S COMBINED FOLK TUNES AND ELECTRIC GUITARS WITH POLITICAL MESSAGES.

## Connect!

FIND OUT HOW THIS ARTIST SHOCKED HIS AUDIENCE IN Q53.

**BOB DYLAN** (born in 1941). This American star's record *Blowin' in the Wind* (1962) became an anthem for young people in America, and gave birth to "protest music," a style which commented on what was happening in the world. Songs were written about war, religion and politics.

**HAIR** The 1967 musical *Hair* was based around American youth rebelling against society during the Vietnam war (1957–75).

**JOHN LENNON** (1940–80). When working as a solo artist, John Lennon wrote many songs with anti-war messages, such as *Give Peace a Chance* (1969), *Imagine* (1971) and *Happy Xmas (War is Over)* (1972).

QUESTION

# 47 Have people always danced to music?

## Probably, yes.

DANCE AND MUSIC WERE IMPORTANT IN EARLY RITUALS AND CEREMONIES...

| MAKING CROPS GROW | CELEBRATING A BIRTH | HEALING THE SICK | DEFEATING ENEMIES |
|---|---|---|---|

PREHISTORIC PAINTINGS SHOWING DANCERS HAVE BEEN FOUND ON CAVE WALLS IN AFRICA AND SOUTHERN EUROPE. THESE ARE MORE THAN 20,000 YEARS OLD.

### ☆ THE WALTZ

THE WALTZ, WHICH DEVELOPED FROM A GERMAN AND AUSTRIAN FOLK DANCE CALLED A LÄNDLER, WAS POPULAR IN THE 19TH CENTURY. IT CAUSED A SCANDAL AT THE TIME, BECAUSE IT ALLOWED CLOSE CONTACT BETWEEN MEN AND WOMEN. **JOHANN STRAUSS** (1825–99), FROM VIENNA, WROTE MUSIC ESPECIALLY FOR THE WALTZ.

### ☆ BALLET

MUSIC AND DANCE COME TOGETHER IN BALLET. THE RUSSIAN COMPOSER **PETER ILICH TCHAIKOVSKY** (1840–93) WROTE THE SCORES FOR THE BALLET *SWAN LAKE* AND *THE SLEEPING BEAUTY*. THE MUSIC REFLECTS THE MOVEMENTS AND ACTIONS TAKING PLACE ON THE STAGE AND STILL ACCOMPANIES MODERN PRODUCTIONS.

### ☆ ASIAN TRADITIONS

IN ASIA, TRADITIONAL THEATRE COMBINES DANCE, MUSIC, PANTOMIME AND SPEECH. INDIAN TEMPLE DANCES USE *MUDRAS*, OR HAND GESTURES, AND SONGS TO RELATE HINDU LEGENDS.

### ☆ AFRICAN FESTIVALS

DANCING TO MUSIC IS AN IMPORTANT PART OF AFRICAN FESTIVALS THAT CELEBRATE OCCASIONS LIKE THE HARVEST, BIRTHS AND YOUNG PEOPLE BECOMING ADULTS. IN SOME DANCES EACH PART OF THE DANCER'S BODY FOLLOWS THE RHYTHM OF A DIFFERENT INSTRUMENT.

| WESTERN POPULAR MUSIC HAS INSPIRED MANY DANCE CRAZES |
|---|
| 1940s JIVE |
| 1960s THE TWIST |
| 1970s DISCO |
| 1980s BREAK-DANCING |
| 1990s RAVE |

## Connect!

CHECK OUT Q49 AND Q50 TO DISCOVER HOW MUSIC RELATES TO FASHION.

---

QUESTION

# 48 How does music tell us what is going on in the world?

## People have used music and lyrics to describe the events of their world, and their reaction to those events.

### ☆ FOLK MUSIC

All countries have traditional folk songs, which tell stories about people's everyday lives, their work, homes, battles, children, as well as nature and the seasons. In the 19th century, machinery took over many jobs traditionally done by hand, so people moved to towns looking for work. To stop folk songs being forgotten, some musicians travelled around Europe so that they could write down and record folk songs.

### ☆ RAP

This music developed out of the experiences of young black people living in America. A performer "talks" in rhythm and rhyme, over a background of music which includes electronic drumbeats and scratching (where the needle of a record player is pulled over a record as it is playing). Some stars, such as Ice-T, have become cult heroes, selling millions of records.

## Connect!

WHICH COMPOSERS WERE SO FASCINATED BY FOLK MUSIC THAT THEY TRAVELLED AROUND THEIR COUNTRY COLLECTING IT? SEE Q52.

QUESTION

# 49 How are fashion and music linked?

**Performers, seen on television, in magazines and pictured on their recordings, influence fashion trends and fans' tastes.**

| ☆ ERA | ☆ STYLE AND STARS | | ☆ THE FANS AND "THE LOOK" |
|---|---|---|---|
| 1940s | JAZZ<br>MILES DAVIS<br>DIZZY GILLESPIE<br>CHARLIE PARKER | | MEN WORE BAGGY SUITS, WIDE TIES, FLAMBOYANT SHAWL COLLARS AND TWO-TONE SHOES. |
| 1950s | ROCK 'N' ROLL<br>ELVIS PRESLEY<br>BUDDY HOLLY<br>EDDIE COCHRAN | | MEN HAD LONG SIDEBURNS AND GREASED HAIR, TIGHT BLACK TROUSERS, BOOTLACE TIES, CRÊPE-SOLED SUEDE SHOES OR POINTED BLACK LEATHER BOOTS. |
| 1970s | GLAM ROCK<br>DAVID BOWIE<br>GARY GLITTER<br>SWEET | | BRIGHTLY COLORED MAKEUP FOR MEN AND WOMEN, OUTRAGEOUS AND SPECTACULAR COSTUMES, BOLD OR METALLIC COLORS, BLEACHED OR DYED HAIR, LARGE PLATFORM-SOLED BOOTS. |

QUESTION

# 50 Can we tell what the music is like by looking at the audience?

## Sometimes, yes.

Some people behave and dress in a way that reflects their passion for the music they like. Fans may copy the performers, then add to the "look." Their haircuts, clothes, jewellery, make-up, and even the way they stand and behave, all give us clues to their musical tastes.

THE HEAVY METAL GROUP →

THE HEAVY METAL FANS →

**Connect!** WHICH INNOVATION MADE PERFORMERS MORE AWARE OF WHAT THEY LOOKED LIKE? SEE Q51.

QUESTION

# 51 How have technological advances affected "live" music?

**In the past, all music used to be "live," or performed in real time to real people. Technology has changed this.**

| DATE | INVENTION |
|---|---|
| 1877 | PHONOGRAPH |
| 1887 | FLAT-DISC GRAMOPHONE |
| 1895 | RADIO |
| 1929 | TELEVISION |
| 1948 | LONG PLAYING RECORD |
| 1956 | VIDEO RECORDER |
| 1960 | COMMUNICATIONS SATELLITE |
| 1963 | CASSETTE TAPE RECORDER |
| 1982 | COMPACT DISC SYSTEM |
| 1983 | SATELLITE TV |

### ☆ 12TH CENTURY
Around the 12th century, in medieval Europe, minstrels travelled around the countryside playing in royal courts. In France, these performers were known as troubadours (trouvères). They usually accompanied themselves on the harp or lyre.

### ☆ 18TH CENTURY
In the 18th century, concert halls and opera houses were built. People started to pay money to listen to music and audiences began to grow.

### ☆ 20TH CENTURY
Today, music is still played "live" worldwide. Street musicians, or buskers, entertain the public in return for donations of money. Famous stars play concerts at large venues throughout the world. But there are now other ways that fans can hear music.

### ☆ IMPACT OF INVENTIONS...
● Music is accessible to more people. You can listen to it when you want to and wherever you like.
● Videos accompanying popular songs mean that musicians need to be more aware of their image and "look."
● Live concerts are filmed, then broadcast on television around the world. The size of the audience is increased dramatically.

**Connect!** HOW BIG WAS THE LARGEST AUDIENCE FOR ONE EVENT? SEE Q52.

# 52 Is it a good or bad thing that satellites can beam musical events around the world?

Music can be used to motivate people to care and give, but some countries are losing their traditional sounds and styles as Western popular music begins to dominate their airwaves.

## ☆ SUCCESS STORY—*LIVE AID*

**VENUES:** LONDON AND PHILADELPHIA **DATE:** 13 JULY 1985
Almost one-third of the world's population tuned into the *Live Aid* concerts. That's an estimated audience of around 1.5 billion people. Pictures were beamed around the globe by 12 satellites. Musician **BOB GELDOF** (born 1952) organized the two concerts to bring to the world's attention the devastating famines in Ethiopia and other African countries. The concerts raised over $60 million to buy food and vital supplies.

The Hungarians **BELA BARTOK** (1881–1945) and **ZOLTAN KODALY** (1882–1967) travelled round Hungary and Romania collecting the music of the people. Folk musicians would sing and play into a tape recorder for them. The composers then listened to the recordings and wrote them in musical notation. In this way they collected about 15,000 tunes. Their aim was to preserve folk traditions by using these melodies and rhythms in their own compositions.

**Connect!** COULD TRADITIONAL METHODS OF MAKING MUSIC DIE OUT BECAUSE SO MANY MUSICIANS USE COMPUTERS? SEE Q55.

# 53 Can music shock?

Music and musicians can alarm an audience by producing sounds or performances that are unexpected.

## ☆ EXPERIMENTING WITH SOUND

The Austrian composer **ARNOLD SCHOENBERG** (1874–1951) developed a new style of music called "atonal" music. He thought that notes were free and did not need to follow the rules of Western classical music. His 1912 work *Pierrot Lunaire* ("Moonstruck Pierrot") featured 21 poems about blood, skulls and corpses set to music. The performer sang the piece in a voice which hovered halfway between speaking and singing. One critic wrote: "If this is music then I pray to my Creator not to let me hear it again."

**Prove It!**

Imagine a four-story house where the kitchen is on the ground floor and the bedroom is on the top floor. But suppose you came home each day and found that the rooms had switched floors? That's how confusing people found atonal music, because they couldn't predict it.

## ☆ CHALLENGING TRADITIONS

The American **JOHN CAGE** was among the first to use a prepared piano, where objects are placed between the strings to alter the sound. In his piece *4'33"* (1952) a pianist sits at a piano for four minutes and 33 seconds without playing a note. His music is often written down in an unconventional manner. He composed *Atlas Eclipticalis* (1961) by plotting the positions of the stars on paper and converting them into musical sounds.

# 54

## Why do some people become legends?

(AND OTHERS ARE FORGOTTEN?)

### Composers are remembered if their music is passed on from one generation to another by their fans and other musicans.

#### ☆ THEY MAY...

COMPOSE MUSIC THAT IS POPULAR IN THEIR DAY.

BE VERY SKILLED AT PLAYING AN INSTRUMENT.

INSPIRE A NATION WITH NEW AND EXCITING SOUNDS.

● **MOZART** composed some of the world's most famous music. Although he sold his compositions, gave music lessons and performances, he never earned enough money to support his family and died a very poor man at the age of 35.

● Some of today's composers and pop stars, such as **ANDREW LLOYD WEBBER** and **MICHAEL JACKSON**, reach large audiences and have become famous and wealthy.

**ASK YOURSELF...**
WHICH MUSIC CREATED TODAY WILL BE REMEMBERED IN TWO HUNDRED YEARS TIME, AND WHY?

#### ☆ DELIVERING THE UNEXPECTED

**1** IN 1913, A BALLET BY **IGOR STRAVINSKY** (1882–1971), CALLED *THE RITE OF SPRING*, CAUSED A RIOT. THE AUDIENCE WAS UPSET BY THE MUSIC'S IRREGULAR RHYTHMS AND UNPREDICTABLE MELODIES.

**2** UNTIL THE MID–1960S, FOLK SINGERS ALWAYS ACCOMPANIED THEMSELVES ON ACOUSTIC INSTRUMENTS. IN 1965, **BOB DYLAN** SHOCKED THE AUDIENCE BY WALKING ON STAGE WITH AN ELECTRIC GUITAR. HE ALSO CHANGED THE TEMPO OF THE MUSIC AND HIS SINGING STYLE.

#### ☆ ALIENATING SOCIETY

Musicians may represent ideas which are alien to most of the people in that society. In the 1970s, "punk" music and fashion shocked Britain. The **SEX PISTOLS** caused uproar by putting a picture of Queen Elizabeth II with a safety pin through her nose on the cover of their record *God Save the Queen.*

---

IF WE CAN PROGRAM COMPUTERS TO COMPOSE AND PLAY MUSIC...

# 55

## What will happen to music?

### Music will continue to develop, guided by musicians with skill and vision.

Electronic instruments can reproduce the sounds of traditional instruments. Synthesizers can copy musical sounds and create new ones. Computers can memorize patterns of sound and make new patterns out of that memory.

**But...**

MUSIC EXPRESSES HUMAN FEELINGS AND MOODS.

MUSIC IS ABOUT CREATING A BOND BETWEEN THE MUSICIAN, THE MUSIC AND THE AUDIENCE.

MUSIC GROWS OUT OF THE TRADITIONS AND EXPERIENCES OF THE PEOPLE WHO MAKE IT.

### Machines cannot do this. Music needs people!

#### ☆ LIMITLESS POSSIBILITIES...

**NITIN SAWHNEY**'s work combines the musical traditions and instruments of many cultures. He is influenced by Asian and Caribbean music and jazz. In his record called *Spirit Dance* (1994) he uses guitars, keyboards and computers as well as Indian tablas and flutes. The result is an exotic and innovative mixture of the East and the West.

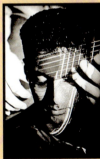

### Connections!

● The music of the planet filled the air long before humans arrived. We need music because it helps us to communicate with each other and understand each other. Music will develop and change as society moves on, and we will use it to solve our problems and to entertain ourselves. Music will always be around us.

# Connections!
# MUSIC
## Index

☆ **ACKNOWLEDGEMENTS** Front cover: Mary Evans: tl. Ron Giling: bl. Mauritius/Ace Photos: cl. PA News: bc. Redferns/Pankaj Shah: bl. Rex Features: tl. Penny Tweedie/Panos Pictures: cr. Zefa: c. Back Cover: Clive Barda/P.A.L: tr. Steve Niedorf/Image Bank: cl. Redferns/David Redfern: cr, Richie Aaron: tl. P1 @Caroline Grimshaw. P3 Redferns: bl. Chris Stowers/Panos Pictures: cr. P4 Neil Cooper/Panos Pictures: tr. Mary Evans: trc. Redferns: tl, tlc. P5 Redferns: cr. P6 Luiz Claudio Marigo/Bruce Coleman Ltd: bl, R. Glover: bc. Rex Features: tr. P7 Clive Barda/P.A.L: c. Gary Price/Ace Photos: background r. Redferns: br. Rex Features: cr. P8 Barnaby's Picture Library: bcr. Bubbles/Loisjoy Thurston: bcl, bcll. Mary Evans: bl, br, bcbl. Redferns: bc. Rex Features: bcrr, bcrr. P9 Barnaby's Picture Library: bl. Panos Pictures: tr. Rex Features: br. Pictor International: background. Zefa: tr. P10 Barnaby's Picture Library: tl. Rex Features: tr. P11 Clive Barda/P.A.L: tr. Rex Features: cl. P12 Image Bank: cl, cr. P13 Jonathon Fisher/P.A.L: cl, br. Mauritius/Ace Photos: cr. Redferns: tl, tc, tr, ct. Tony Stone: ct. P14 Visual Arts: c. Bridgeman Art Library: cr. P15 Christie's Images: bl. Steve Gillet/P.A.L: tl. Redferns: bc. Ray Stevenson/Retna: br. Tony Stone: background bl. P16 Clive Barda/P.A.L: bcr, Jane Mont: bcl. Brett Froomer/Image Bank: tl. Steve Niedorf: tc. Ann Ronan/Image Select: bl. Redferns: tr, br. Telegraph Colour Library: background b. P17 Jonathon Fisher/P.A.L: tr, Steve Gillet: bl. Image Bank: cr. Redferns: br. P18 Clive Barda/P.A.L: tc. Redferns: bc. P19 Hulton Deutsch: br. Telegraph Colour Library: background. P20 Tony Stone: background. P22 Clive Barda/P.A.L: tl. FPG Int./Robert Harding: bc. Redferns: bl, tr. Tony Stone: br. P23 London Features: br. Linda Rich/P.A.L: tr. P24 PA News: tr. P25 Steve Gillett/P.A.L: bl. Image Bank: background. Redferns: cr, bl, br. P26 Fine Art Photographs: bl. Redferns: cr, cl, br. Tony Stone: bl, background. P27 Fritz Curzon/P.A.L: bl. Redferns: br. P28 CM Dixon: tr. Redferns: cl, cll, br. Tony Stone: cr, crr. P29 Redferns. P30 Clive Barda/P.A.L: br. Redferns: tc. P31 Redferns: bl, br.
Every effort has been made to acknowledge correctly and contact the source and/or copyright holder of each picture and Two-Can Publishing apologies for any unintentional errors or omissions which will be corrected in future editions of this book.